Itty Bitty Ar

ITTY BITTY GUPPIES

By Alex Lumpy

Gareth Stevens
Publishing

Please visit our website, www.garethstevens.com. For a free color catalog of all our high-quality books, call toll free 1-800-542-2595 or fax 1-877-542-2596.

Library of Congress Cataloging-in-Publication Data

Lumpy, Alex.
Itty bitty guppies / by Alex Lumpy.
  p. cm. — (Itty bitty animals)
Includes index.
ISBN 978-1-4339-9884-3 (pbk.)
ISBN 978-1-4339-9885-0 (6-pack)
ISBN 978-1-4339-9882-9 (library binding)
1. Guppies — Juvenile literature. I. Title.
SF458.G8 L86 2014
639.3757—dc23

First Edition

Published in 2014 by
Gareth Stevens Publishing
111 East 14th Street, Suite 349
New York, NY 10003

Copyright © 2014 Gareth Stevens Publishing

Editor: Ryan Nagelhout
Designer: Nicholas Domiano

Photo credits: Cover, pp. 1, 21, 24 (fry) Sailesh Patel/Shutterstock.com; p. 5 © iStockphoto.com/scottyspics; p. 7 Nikolay Dimitrov - ecobo/Shutterstock.com; pp. 9, 23 bluehand/Shutterstock.com; p. 11, 24 (stripe) Andrew Illyasov/E+/Getty Images; p. 13 subin pumsom/Shutterstock.com; p. 15 LDiza/Shutterstock.com; p. 17 Kerstin Klaassen/E+/Getty Images; p. 19 Richard Boll/Photographer's Choice/Getty Images; p. 23 Mijang Ka/Flickr/Getty Images; p. 24 (water) iStockphoto/Thinkstock.com.

All rights reserved. No part of this book may be reproduced in any form without permission in writing from the publisher, except by a reviewer.

Printed in the United States of America

CPSIA compliance information: Batch #CW14GS: For further information contact Gareth Stevens, New York, New York at 1-800-542-2595.

Contents

Guppies are little fish!

They like to swim
in water.

They are full of color.

Some have stripes.

They were discovered
in 1866.

Boy guppies are smaller than girls.

Girl guppies do not lay eggs. They give birth to live babies.

Baby guppies can swim right away!

A baby guppy is called a fry.

Guppies make
great pets.

Words to Know

fry

stripes

water

Index

24